THE TEN SECRETS

OF

LIVING YOUR DREAM

THE TEN SECRETS

OF

LIVING YOUR DREAM

Leyla Atwill

Bhakti Yogini West
Maui, Hawaii

THE TEN SECRETS OF LIVING YOUR DREAM

Published by Bhakti Yogini West
P.O. Box 1622
Kihei, HI
96753

Printed in the United States of America

LCCN 2003090122
ISBN 0-9726705-1-3

First Edition

For Frank

You are my dream of a husband come true.

CONTENTS

A NOTE TO READERS

Seek the advice of appropriate professionals when you are planning to make dramatic changes in your life. The information in this book cannot replace that advice.

NOTES

INTRODUCTION

Whether your dream is to have more money, a beautiful and healthy body, a loving relationship, or to retire early, your dream *can* come true. If you've tried and failed to achieve your dream there are keys that will open the gates that have been blocking you.

The Ten Secrets you will learn in this book are the keys that opened the gates for me. In my journey towards realizing my dreams I found that it wasn't enough to visualize, set goals, think positive, and work hard. Finding the keys that would open the heavenly gates of my dreams became my lifelong mission.

I searched hundreds of books of ancient as well as contemporary wisdom. My travels led me to Eastern and Western spiritual teachings, psychology, modern-day science, and to the practical wisdom of hard-edged business thinkers.

The Ten Secrets are the synthesis of the wisdom I have gathered from three decades of trial and error, research, and meditation on how to bring dreams to reality. You will find the wisdom of these many sources distilled to their essence in The Ten Secrets. They are the treasures of my life-long quest. By learning these secrets you will be spared from the mistakes that I made and walk an unobstructed path to manifesting your heart's desire.

I have come from a humble and difficult beginning in life and have lived to see some of my most cherished dreams come true. I have traveled to exotic lands, lived in beautiful places, and had careers that would not have been possible if I had not believed in my dreams. If I had not believed in my dreams I would not be living the idyllic life I live today. I now live on the island of Maui in Hawaii with my prince of a husband, Frank. My dream of having the leisure time to write this book has come true.

My life is filled with great joy and blessings. This book is my way of sharing the treasures of what I've learned on that journey so that you, my friend and fellow traveler, may travel a smoother road than mine. May the gates of heaven open to you.

HOW TO USE THIS BOOK

Begin by purchasing a notebook specifically for working with the Ten Secrets. You can also use your own diary or journal if you already keep one. Just devise a way for marking your dream manifesting notes so that they stand apart from the rest of your entries. This way you can refer to them easily in the future.

Your journal will be the bridge from your dream world to your real world as well as a companion along the way. It will be the garden in which your dreams will grow into reality. In it you will write what dreams you want to realize, work out obstacles that may be standing in your way, define practical actions to take, and any revelations you may have.

When you look at your Dream Manifesting Journal after your dream has become real it will function as an affirmation that you can and did bring your dream to earth. This will make it easier for you to manifest future dreams because you will have overcome the doubt that living your dreams was possible.

As you work with the Secrets you will notice that I use the terms "manifesting your heart's desire" and "living your dream" interchangeably. This is because they are essentially the same. Your heart communicates its desires to you through your dreams and daydreams. If you find you are confused about what you really want in life your dreams and daydreams will point the way clearly.

Take your time with learning the Secrets. If one Secret is more difficult for you than the others, just relax and spend a little more time on it. You may even decide to skip it and come back to it later. When you have trouble with one of the Secrets it is an indication that mastering it will dissolve a wall that has blocked your dream from coming true. Patience in working with that particular Secret will clear the way for you.

The *I Ching* is an ancient book of wisdom that the Chinese have used for thousands of years. It explored the meanings of events in their lives and ways of handling them. *I Ching* means "The Book of Changes." It is a guide on how to navigate the changes in life with wisdom. When you encounter an obstacle, The *I Ching* counsels you to be like flowing water when its course is blocked. A river, for example, when it encounters a dam will pause while it builds its energy. Once it builds enough energy the river flows effortlessly over the dam. In working with the Secrets, if you have difficulty you too can pause and build your energy until you flow over the obstacle naturally. This may mean giving yourself extra time with that particular Secret or coming back to it later.

In Hatha Yoga when you want to master a pose you relax and breathe until your body eases into the posture. In manifesting your dreams, you relax and breathe through your obstacles. In this way your dreams flow into your real world naturally.

Once you've manifested your dream you'll find that going through the Secrets to manifest new dreams becomes progressively easier. The first few times around take the most patience and energy but you'll find your confidence is stronger every time another dream manifests. You'll eventually find that living your dreams comes naturally to you.

After you've realized some of your dreams you may find that people ask you how you did it. Take the time to explain as best as you can. If you don't have the patience then just have them read this book. In this way, by living your dream you make it possible for others to live theirs. You'll be a channel for heaven to come down to earth. The more you help others prosper, the more you will prosper. Prosperity means more than having money. It also means having love, health, wisdom, and all the other intangible good things in life. The Bible's Golden Rule about doing for others as you would have them do for you is a great prosperity secret.

Last, be patient and kindly to yourself as you go through the steps. Your greatest dream holds the seed of your greatest self and is meant to come true. Patience and your concentrated energy will get you there.

NOTES

SECRET ONE

Realize your unity with Infinite Intelligence.

To bring your dreams to reality you begin from a sense of wholeness within yourself. You acknowledge your unity with Infinite Intelligence and therefore with all things. If you skip this first Secret you haven't plugged into your power source and your success will be limited.

Whether you call this power source God, Higher Self, Infinite Intelligence, Nature, Goddess, Buddha, Brahman, or The Tao is not important. What is important is that you have a comfortable concept for this power source and that you feel connected with it.

Great religions, spiritual teachers, and illumined philosophers remind us of our unity with Infinite

Intelligence, the world and all its creatures. They remind us that coming from one source we are all made of the same essence, the same life power. The easiest way to feel this connection is to open your heart and mind to this Infinite Intelligence and to the world around you. This is what is meant by the ancient instruction that asks us first to seek the Kingdom of Heaven and thereby have all good things added to us. It's a way of saying that we need to plug into our power source, which is Infinite Intelligence.

If you have trouble opening your mind to this connection you might read books such as Fritjof Capra's *Tao of Physics* or Danah Zohar's *Quantum Self*. Both of these books refer to the findings of respected physicists such as Werner Heisenberg, Niels Bohr, and David Bohm. The new physics is beginning to indicate a mysterious unity between us and the manifested universe.

In his book, *Physics and Philosophy*, renowned physicist Werner Heisenberg explained how observing an object changes that object. Heisenberg wrote that a hard separation between the world and us could not be possible.

Other sciences such as ecology also point to the complex interrelatedness of everything on our planet. Science is beginning to confirm what great religions and ancient wisdom paths have always taught—that we are connected with everything in the manifested universe in a way that transcends our ability to discern that connection with our five senses.

Once you know your unity with the Source and the very fabric of life you then realize your own personal worth and value. You realize that you are an important thread in the fabric of life and without you, life would be lessened. You know this most clearly when a loved one dies and you feel the painfully empty space they leave behind. You too would leave an empty space.

Not admitting your personal worth and value is one of the greatest obstacles in realizing your dreams. When you know your worth you begin from a stance of wholeness and strength. You are supported by Infinite Intelligence because you are an important part of the ecology of life.

If you begin from a sense of separation from your Source and the world you are left with only your own limited personal resources. It makes you feel you have to know everything and that you can't acquire what your heart desires because you don't know how. You've forgotten that you have a greater intelligence than your conscious mind at your disposal. This greater intelligence performs the most complex physiological processes to keep you breathing, digesting and your heart beating. If you needed to consciously know how these processes worked you would not survive an hour.

When you know you have access to Infinite Intelligence your information resources are immensely expanded. You can open your mind to the information you need. Infinite Intelligence works through the world of people and circumstances. You find yourself guided to answers like animals are guided to their migrating grounds. The information can come through your natural connections in the world. Books come your way, friends have the answers you need, or you find what you need on the Internet.

You can also connect to Infinite Intelligence and the information you need by being receptive to your subconscious self. I prefer the term "deeper self" because this part of you is much more accessible than the term "subconscious" implies. Infinite Intelligence stores all the physiological information you need to stay alive in this deeper self. Prompted by your deeper self, you feel urges to go to a certain place, take a class, or meet a particular person. Infinite Intelligence communicates to you through this deeper self through hunches, or by sending you a revelation when you are meditating or daydreaming.

This Infinite Intelligence oversees the biological processes that keep you alive. It is intelligent enough to orchestrate the intricate interrelatedness of nature's ecology. Its greater intelligence is available to us if we are receptive to it. It can give us the information we need to live our dreams.

SECRET ONE ACTIONS

-1-

Remember a time when you felt whole, complete, joyful, and connected to all of life and Infinite Intelligence. Remember a time when you felt your personal worth and value.

What part of your body felt this experience? What sensations did you have? Did it feel like an open, expansive sensation in your chest, or perhaps a tingling somewhere in your body? Did you see colors or shapes? Did you see an image or picture? Perhaps you saw and felt a sun shining inside of your body. What keywords describe the experience? This is your feeling experience of Infinite Intelligence, your connection to all of life, and your personal worth. By reproducing the feelings in your body, remembering the colors and shapes, and saying your keywords you can feel this connection to Infinite Intelligence at any time.

Example: You feel an open and relaxed sensation in the middle of your chest and solar plexus.

You see a circle of golden light around these areas. Your keywords might be "opening, profound well-being, I am worthy."

-2-

Start a practice that attunes you to Infinite Intelligence. That practice might be meditation, contemplative walks, or simply breathing deeply and quietly. Find a practice that you enjoy and that you can do routinely. The important thing is to quiet your mind so that you can receive revelations about living your dream from your Infinite Intelligence. One of India's greatest instructions on meditation is *Patanjali's Yoga Sutras*. It tells you that Infinite Intelligence is not outside of you but within you. It instructs you to still your turbulent mind so that you can perceive the presence of Infinite Intelligence within. You do this by calming and quieting, yourself. Then your mind and emotions become a still, clear lake and you can see to the bottom easily, you perceive the Infinite Intelligence more clearly.

Do your chosen practice each day. Practice your feeling connection with Infinite Intelligence that you've just learned as well. Doing this each day will allow Infinite Intelligence to guide you in living your dream.

SECRET ONE AFFIRMATIONS

Affirmations are statements of truth that will replace thoughts, feelings, and attitudes that are limiting you.

I will suggest affirmations for each of the Secrets. You can change the wording or use affirmations you create yourself. Phrases from sacred

21

scriptures such as the Bible or India's *Upanishads* can be very powerful. Great literature such as Shakespeare's works or even song lyrics are good sources for affirmations that reverberate with truth for you. You will notice that the affirmations I suggest are in the present tense and use positive language:

My mind and heart are open to the Infinite Intelligence within me.

I have great worth and value just being myself.

Infinite Intelligence guides me perfectly in making my dream real.

I am whole and complete. My dream is already real within me.

SECRET TWO

Decide on what your heart desires and make a commitment to living it.

In order to live your dream you will need a strong and prolonged focus. The easiest way to sustain concentration and focus is to choose what has real meaning for you, what your heart truly desires. Oddly, we can sometimes feel confused about what we want. If this is so, ask yourself what your ideals are for yourself and the world. What would you love to be or do?

Thomas J. Stanley, Ph.D., author of the *Millionaire Mind*, did studies on the characteristics of millionaires. He found that a love for their work was a powerful contributor to a millionaire's success. When you love something it is much easier to concentrate on it and maintain your focus.

You can use your Manifesting Journal to work out what your dream is in writing. Skip the first few pages of your journal so that when you decide, you can make a title page for the whole notebook. Wait until you've gone through the processes in this section before writing the title page.

If you decide from any other place than your heart and what has real meaning for you your success will be limited. You will obtain your aim but you will not have a sense of real fulfillment in the end. As you choose your heart's desire keep in mind that because of your unity with all of life, any desire you have to harm anyone will harm you in the same measure. By the same token, your desire to prosper the world will also prosper you.

You may find that you have several dreams and desires. Make a list. Define each one as simply and clearly as possible. Now number them in order of importance. You can work on one of these at a time or you may find it easier to state one aim that includes all of them. For example, you may have the following desires in this order of importance:

1. To be vibrantly attractive and healthy
2. To have a loving relationship
3. To have plenty of money

You can work on one at a time beginning with number 1 or you can summarize all three in a single statement. For example, if you decide to work on one at a time, your statement could be "I am vibrantly attractive and healthy." If you decide to summarize all three in a single aim your statement could be "I am vibrantly attractive and healthy, enjoying a loving relationship and I have plenty of money."

Write your statement in the present tense. Use the words "I AM" or "I HAVE." This will give your deeper self the message that this is a present reality, not a mere hope for the future. Now that you've decided on what you desire, make your statement of intention. Begin your statement with the phrase, "I focus all of my energy in the following," and then write your statement. For example, "I focus all of my energy in the following: I am vibrantly healthy and attractive, enjoying a loving relationship, and have plenty of money."

By clearly stating your dream prefaced with the phrase "I focus all of my energy in the following" you are making a commitment to bringing your dream to reality. Now write your statement on the title page of your Manifesting Journal. Congratulations. Your dream has begun to come true.

Your statement of intent directs your consciousness towards making your dream real. Your consciousness is your personal energy. When you focus your consciousness you are focusing your personal energy. Think of your consciousness as being like the water in a garden hose. Whatever you direct the water on will grow. If you don't state your intention clearly you are giving your energy to whatever your attention happens to light upon. Often you focus your consciousness by worrying. This is like watering weeds or poison oak. You're allowing your consciousness to nurture what you don't want.

As you work with the Secrets you may find that you want to re-word or clarify your statement of your heart's desire. If so, correct it on the title page of your Manifesting Journal. It's important that your statement is written clearly and precisely.

SECRET TWO ACTIONS

-1-

Read your statement once in the morning before getting out of bed and once in the evening before falling asleep. Remind yourself of your heart's desire often during the day.

SECRET TWO AFFIRMATIONS

Use your statement of intention as an affirmation. For example:

I am vibrantly healthy and attractive, enjoying a loving relationship and have lots of money.

SECRET THREE

Unify your conscious mind and your deeper self.
Focus them both on living your dream.

Your conscious mind is your everyday waking consciousness. As you learned in Secret One, your deeper self is often called the subconscious or unconscious self and is naturally connected to Infinite Intelligence. This is how the deeper self knows how to direct the physiological processes needed for you to move an arm, see a sunrise, or taste a lemon. The deeper self is your communication link to Infinite Intelligence.

Because you tend to rely exclusively on your

conscious mind it is forced to act without the support of your deeper self. As a consequence you cut yourself off from the support of Infinite Intelligence. This can cause you to feel anxious if you do not consciously know how to manifest your dreams and desires.

In reality, the conscious mind relies on the deeper self to negotiate the simplest of everyday actions. If you want to cross a street the deeper self automatically directs the processes for gauging distances of cars, interpreting traffic signals, and adjusting your walking speed. You simply set your intention to cross the street and your deeper self handles the rest. If you had to consciously direct all of your physical processes you wouldn't be able to cross the street or even get out of bed in the morning.

Your deeper self responds to your conscious self's directions. It also responds to what you imagine, think, and feel. If you tell yourself that you're not feeling well you start feeling run down and more susceptible to a cold. You can tell yourself you don't enjoy parties so you feel uncomfortable when you go to one. You can think you are clumsy and find yourself always knocking things over. You can also tell yourself that your dreams are possible and find opportunities opening up for you that you never saw before.

When Infinite Intelligence communicates through your deeper self to your conscious self you may feel "prompted" or "urged" to take particular actions. You may have a dream or daydream about what to do next. You may have a hunch, an idea may just "occur" to you, or you might have a brilliant revelation that seems to come from nowhere. When you ignore these communications from your deeper self you are missing valuable information for making your dream real.

When your conscious self is in communication

with Infinite Intelligence through your deeper self it has much greater power to manifest your dream. When you deny your conscious mind this support you are forcing it to draw from the limited resource of what it consciously knows. You are denying it access to the powerful reservoir of information that can bring your dream to reality.

To bring your dream to the real world you need to *consciously* direct your deeper self. Too often your directions to your deeper self are negative. You tell yourself you're not intelligent enough, you're not attractive enough, you're unworthy. These are directions that your deeper self acts on just as it acts on your intention to cross a street. Your deeper self is completely responsive to the directions you give it and this is why it seems so difficult to manage. You may think you want to be successful in your career but at the same time you are also telling your deeper self that you don't have what it takes to be successful. The deeper self now has two instructions that conflict. The result is that your personal power is divided. Part of you is doing everything you can to be successful and the other part is busily sabotaging you. In the days of King Arthur and the Round Table it was said that a knight that was not true could not win. This is a way of saying that if you are conflicted in your intentions your personal power is divided and so you are working with only half your power.

In Secret Two you united your conscious mind with your deeper self by listening to your heart to define the dream you want to realize. Your conscious self then sets the direction for your deeper self by making a clear statement that would focus all of your energy in living that dream. Secret Three keeps the channel of communication open between these two parts of you. Instead of these aspects of you

29

functioning alone or in conflict with each other they are now a unified force for making your dream a reality.

Chin-Ning Chu is an internationally respected business thinker and strategist. In her book, *Do Less Achieve More*, she writes that the Harvard Business School and the leading European business school, INSEAD, agree that meditation and intuition are cutting-edge business tools for today's decision-makers. Meditation and intuition are simply methods of keeping your conscious self and deeper self unified.

SECRET THREE ACTIONS

-1-

Be aware of the directions you are giving to your deeper self. Notice if your directions are negative or positive

-2-

Listen to your intuition by respecting hunches, urges, or inspirations that come to you. Write them in your Manifesting Journal. Use discrimination when you assess which hunches to act on. With experience, you will be able to discern when you should act on an urge and when it is simply a fleeting impulse.

-3-

Pay attention to any dreams that seem important. Write them in your manifesting journal. It doesn't matter whether you understand the dream or not. Writing the dream in your journal gives your deeper self the message that you are open to understanding its communications. If it is truly important that you understand the dream your deeper self will reveal the meaning to you at the right time.

-4-

In the Secret One Actions you chose a practice such as meditation or contemplative walking. This will keep the channel of communication open as you continue the practice. Write any revelations that occur to you during your practice in your Manifesting Journal. Assess these revelations and act on the ones that seem practical.

AFFIRMATIONS

My conscious mind and my deeper self work together in living my dream now.

NOTES

SECRET FOUR

Imagine that your dream is real now.

In order to have something, you first need to *be* the person that would have that particular thing. If you want to have a loving relationship you must first be someone who is willing to make adjustments in your life for the beloved. If you want a slim body you must be someone who is comfortable in a slim body and does the things that maintain a slim body. If you want more money you have to be someone who feels worthy of more money.

To be this new person you need to use your imagination to create an image or a vision of yourself

33

as this new person. Imagine you are living this new image of yourself in the present. You do this by acting as if or pretending that you are already this new person. If you want a trimmer body you would act as if you enjoyed being physically active, that you enjoyed eating healthy food, and that you found overeating physically uncomfortable. If you wanted to have a joyful new career, act as if you already have the career, live your day as if you are doing the things that you'd be doing in your new work.

Who and what you are emerges from your deeper self in response to what you imagine for yourself. Imagination is the ability to create an image or vision in your mind. If you do not consciously have an image or vision for yourself your deeper self will take suggestions from what friends or family would like you to be, or from what society and advertising say you should be. A strong image or vision for yourself is a powerful motivator. You might see an image of yourself sailing to Tahiti, being the CEO of your own company, or being a humanitarian saint like Mother Theresa. Conversely, if you don't choose a vision for yourself, your friends, family, or society might tell you that you should live in the same city all you life and that you can never be anyone different from who you are now.

The Qabalah is the wisdom and philosophy of the ancient Hebrew mystics. One of its most beautiful tenets is that we as human beings are emanations of the Divine Source, and as its spiritual children we are to emulate the perfection of our divine parentage to emerge into our truest selves. When you dream of being someone or having something your deeper self is seeking to bring you closer to the greater self that you are destined to be. Your vision or dream is the seed of your greater self. In other words, what you dream of being is already potentially real within you. Your true self is simply waiting to emerge from inside of you. Understanding this will make it easier for you to act as if you already are who you desire to be.

Always imagine that your dream is real in the *present.* If you imagine it in the future you will find that your dream never quite manifests in the here and now.

When I was 18 years old I was sitting at a bus stop in downtown Oakland in California. It was a dismal, gray morning and I was going to work at a job that I merely endured. My life looked as bleak and colorless as the drab city around me. As I sat there I imagined I was in a beautiful town by the ocean. It was bright with flowers and sunlight. I imagined myself a career woman. Years later I found myself living and working in Santa Barbara, California, one of the most beautiful cities in the world. It was a job that fulfilled many hopes and dreams for me. My youthful vision had become a reality despite its improbability at the time I imagined it.

So if it feels like using your imagination this way is simply a flight of fantasy, remember that to imagine is to create an image or concept in your mind. Remind yourself of all the marvelous things we have today because someone had imagined or dreamed them despite seemingly impossible odds. Think of the Wright brothers imagining a flying machine, President Kennedy imagining a man on the moon, and the American founding fathers imagining a land of freedom and liberty.

SECRET FOUR ACTIONS

-1-

Imagine yourself already living your dream. Say your affirmation of your heart's desire. For example, say to yourself, "I am vibrantly attractive and healthy, enjoying a loving relationship and have lots of money now."

As you say this to yourself notice what it feels like, what do you see and hear around you? What are you doing? What are you feeling and thinking?

As you go through your normal day, act as if or pretend that you are already living your dream.

-2-

Before getting out of bed in the morning and before falling asleep at night you are naturally closer to your deeper self. Say your statement to yourself at these times. Breathe and feel you are one with your heart's desire and not separate from it. Hold a feeling of wholeness and completeness within yourself. This will direct your deeper self to make your dream a current reality.

AFFIRMATIONS

Add the word "now" to the end of your living your dream statement. For example:

"I am vibrantly attractive and healthy, enjoying a loving relationship and have plenty of money NOW."

SECRET FIVE

Choose your thoughts and what you say to yourself consciously.

The Buddha taught that we are made of our thoughts and the Bible agrees when it says "As a man thinketh in his heart so is he." Martin Seligman, PH.D., psychologist and author of the book *Learned Optimism*, writes that one of the most important findings of contemporary psychology is that we can choose how we think.

Thought is what you are saying to yourself. What you say to yourself determines how you feel about yourself and life. If you tell yourself that you are unworthy of love, you will feel unlovable. You will think that having a loving relationship is not possible for you. You will believe that love has passed you by.

Too often you have accepted negative feelings and beliefs without questioning whether they are true or not. You haven't realized that the reason you feel and believe these negative things is simply that you have said them to yourself so often that you now accept them as reality. This is how what we think determines what we experience in life.

If you feel that you aren't attractive, don't have enough money, or that you'll never have a loving relationship, your life will reflect back to you what you think about yourself. You are probably telling yourself that it's impossible for you to feel attractive, that you're unworthy of having more money. You are probably telling yourself a loving mate would put too many demands on you. Everyone has their own set of negative things they say to themselves.

Your deeper self will take what you habitually say to yourself as directions for what you want it to do. You will find that your deeper self moves according to your directions even if they disempower you. If you habitually tell yourself you are worthless your deeper self will arrange to have your life reflect your worthlessness to you. Once your life confronts you with these situations you then take them as proof of your worthlessness.

I know that you are asking, "But how can I change what I really feel and believe is true?" What you feel and believe is the result of what you think and what you think is the result of what you say to yourself. The easiest way to change what you feel and believe is to change what you say to yourself. You change by talking to yourself in a more truthful and uplifting manner.

Your thoughts are composed of your own energy. When you allow your thoughts to stray into negative streams you are allowing your energy and personal power to flow out counter productively. You are watering weeds and poison oak. When you drive a car it will move in the direction you focus on consistently. Your life will move in the direction your thoughts focus on consistently.

If you repeatedly tell yourself your dream is impossible you'll find insurmountable mountains looming in front of you. If instead you tell yourself that your dream is completely possible you will find opportunities opening in front of you. For this reason, it's a good idea to severely question negative statements you say to yourself. Ask yourself if these statements actually have any truth. Have you simply developed a bad habit of saying unpleasant things to yourself? If you think there is some truth to these negative ideas you have about yourself what positive actions can you take? On the other hand, you may find that they are completely inaccurate.

The difference between who you are and who you want to be is in the things you tell yourself. When you take control of what you are saying to yourself you are taking control of your thinking and how you feel about yourself. You will find that you are no longer at the mercy of what you believe about yourself. Instead, you will realize that you can choose the kinds of thoughts that will manifest your heart's desire instead of blocking you from it.

SECRET FIVE ACTIONS

-1-

Make a list of any negative feelings, beliefs and thoughts you are having. Go through each item and realize that it is simply a statement you have made to yourself, and that it is simply a thought. Ask yourself if the statement is actually true. If you do think it is true make another list of why you think it's true. Realize that this second list is also a list of statements you have made to yourself.

-2-

Go through each item on both lists and write a more truthful thought next to it. For example, your negative thought might be "There is no way I can ever retire early." A more truthful thought might be "I haven't actually explored all the possibilities so I really don't know if it's impossible or not. I've assumed it's impossible without doing any research."

AFFIRMATIONS

I choose my thoughts by consciously choosing the things I tell myself.

I can choose what I feel and believe about myself.

SECRET SIX

Concentrate all of your actions on living your dream.

Action connects your inner world of imagination, desire, and thought with the outer everyday world. The actions you take are the bridges that link your dream to the real world. Taking action is what brings your heart's desire to your physical reality.

Think about what physical actions you need to take to make your dream real. What activities does your body need to do? Think about simple actions at first. Let's say you want to have more money. You could buy a book on the characteristics of wealthy people. If you want to have a loving relationship you could make a list of reasons you might be resisting having a mate. If you want to feel more attractive and physically fit you could research different kinds of exercise that would be fun to do every day. Think about simple activities that you are actually willing to do that will move you closer to your dream. As you take action with the easier activities the more difficult ones will eventually seem less challenging.

Each day you have a choice about what activities you do. Choose the activities that bring you closer to your dreams and forego activities that do not seem to contribute. There are those times when you have to engage in activities that don't seem to be getting you closer to your heart's desire. For example, you may want a job that gives you joy each day but you presently have a job that you dislike. Your present job may be a necessary activity until you can create the job you desire. It can provide you with the ability to take your time in creating your new work because you will not be anxious about income.

By choosing what actions to take you are once again directing your energy and focusing it on your heart's desire. When all of your energy is focused in one direction you are like a magnifying glass that concentrates sunlight so that it burns through wood. When that same sunlight is not concentrated it's incapable of burning through paper.

Each day then, concentrate your energy by choosing the activities that will bring you closer to your heart's desire and if possible, forego those activities that do not contribute.

SECRET SIX ACTIONS

-1-

Make a list of actions and activities you need to do. Start with easy activities and work up to the more challenging ones. Separate the items on the list into a list of things to be done now, another list for the near future, and a third list for actions further in the future.

-2-

Each day choose actions from your list to do. Choose the ones that are easiest for you to accomplish.

-3-

Forego, if possible, activities that don't contribute to your dream coming true.

AFFIRMATIONS

Fill in the blank with the dream you want to manifest:

I concentrate all of my actions on being/having_____.

NOTES

SECRET SEVEN

Realize what feelings and thoughts are keeping
you from living your dream now.

Not acknowledging the negative attitudes and
ideas you may be harboring is one of the biggest walls
you encounter when you are manifesting your dream.
When you don't acknowledge these negative attitudes
you are allowing them to act automatically because you
are unconscious of them. Let's say, for example, that
you believe you are unworthy and without value but
you are not consciously aware of this feeling. You
essentially have an automatic instruction to your
deeper self that tells it to make achieving your dream

extremely difficult.

While it is good to have an optimistic focus in life it is unwise to hide negative feelings from yourself. Covering up these painful feelings and thoughts with a positive veneer only delays your dream from flowing naturally into your real world. When you refuse to acknowledge hidden negative attitudes they act automatically to undermine your progress. Positive thinking covering up painful feelings and thoughts will give conflicting messages to your deeper self. This results in an uphill struggle or worse, a complete stalemate so that you never manifest your dream.

You may want a loving mate but secretly feel terrified of being trapped. You have one intention of having a relationship and another intention to avoid entrapment. You find yourself in relationships that never work out.

You may believe you don't have any resistance or hidden negative attitudes to manifesting your dream but you still can't manifest your dream. Many times this is because you don't want to know that you are harboring a particular feeling. For example, you want to have a thriving business but at the same time you are hiding a feeling that you have nothing of real value to offer. You deny what you really feel because you think that to admit this would mean you couldn't move forward in your business. You compensate by working harder and acting more confident but you never truly feel confident. The result is that every bit of progress you make is a struggle. It's as if you are driving your car with the emergency brake on.

Your conscious mind has not wanted to listen to your deeper self. In Secret Three we talked about unifying your conscious mind with your deeper self. If you allow these two parts of yourself to communicate the inner conflict can be healed. Eventually this communication will flow so naturally that conflicts are minimized or avoided altogether.

The Step Seven Actions are important to do slowly and patiently. As you take action in manifesting your dream be aware of any feelings of anxiety or discomfort. These feelings are your deeper self communicating negative feelings that need to be acknowledged and healed.

SECRET SEVEN ACTIONS

-1-

Look at the list of negative things you tell yourself from your Secret Five Actions. Mark the items that cause you the most anxiety and discomfort. You may realize you have negative feelings that you did not put on your list the first time. Add them now. Give yourself a day or two to allow any negative feelings you may have been harboring to surface.

-2-

Make another list of all the reasons you think you *cannot* live your dream.

-3-

The lists you now have are the thoughts and feelings that are keeping you from living your dream now. Allow any further negative thoughts and feelings to surface but do not allow yourself to dwell upon them. In the Secret Eight we will talk about healing these attitudes.

AFFIRMATIONS

I allow myself to consciously know any negative attitudes that I am harboring that are keeping me from living my dream now.

SECRET EIGHT

Heal these negative feelings and thoughts by telling yourself the truth about them and letting them go.

The lists you made in the Secret Seven Actions represent what you believe. Beliefs are made up of thoughts, feelings, and attitudes that you have assumed are true. What you assume to be true will shape your life by limiting what you experience to what you think is possible. Unfortunately, what you assume to be true may not be true at all. You simply haven't taken the time to examine and question these attitudes. While you have been critical towards your abilities and potentials, you have *not* been critical about the beliefs you have assumed to be true.

Your deeper self will carry out your directions even when they are unconscious. It will manifest what you believe even if what you believe is untrue.

In order to move beyond the limited beliefs that are shaping your life you need to tell yourself the truth about the negative beliefs you have been clinging to. As you grow wiser you move from truth to greater truth. Perhaps the beliefs you hold were true when you were less mature, but you are evolving and the old truth no longer serves you. As a child just beginning to walk, the truth was that you needed an adult to help you cross the street. As an adult you have evolved past that need and that old truth.

When you shed your old truths in favor of new, larger truths you are like a snake shedding its old constricting skin for a more flexible new skin. You are a new person with a larger truth that is more fitting for your new life. Like the snake, you need to shed your old, constricting beliefs. The new truth will set you free of old beliefs that have been limiting you.

You tend to see things in a way that supports what you think is true. You do not support things that you do not believe are true. For example, if you believe you are unattractive you will pick out ways the world tells you that you are unattractive. If someone looks at you your assumption is that they think that you are unattractive. If someone tells you how nice you look you think that they are only being polite. Even though there are many events that tell you that you are attractive you will not accept them as true and ignore them completely.

You need to keep this in mind when you look at your lists of negative feelings and beliefs. It can seem that these beliefs are true and that you cannot change them. The fact is that they only seem true because you use only the feedback from the world that substantiates your feelings. You do this by choosing only those experiences that conform to your beliefs. Your conscious mind works like a debater who will only look for information that supports his or her position and ignores any information that does not support it.

Look at your lists again with this truth in mind. Look at each item and see how you have chosen only those experiences in your life that have supported that belief. Notice when you have ignored experiences that did not agree with your belief. Now question whether or not that belief is actually true.

The truth is that if you are seeing yourself with critical, judgmental eyes you are not seeing who you truly are. Critical and judgmental attitudes limit your perception not only of yourself but of the world in general. If your perception is limited you are not seeing the whole truth. You are like a judge in court who chooses to hear only one side's testimonies. To see the truth you need to open your perception. When you see with the limited perception of a critical and judgmental attitude you are seeing only a part of the whole. If you are only seeing part of the whole then you are not seeing the whole truth.

To see with the eyes of love is to see the truth more accurately. Look at each item on your lists. Are you seeing yourself with the whole vision of love or the limited perception of a judgmental and critical attitude?

When you realize the wisdom of seeing with the eyes of love you can then see your own worth and value more clearly. What gives something value is how much we appreciate it. If we do not appreciate something we do not give it value. To appreciate also means to be conscious of something. When you "appreciate" someone's position you are saying you understand and are conscious of their situation. When you are able to appreciate yourself you are able to understand and be conscious of your worth.

If you criticize and negatively judge yourself you have not learned to truly appreciate your own qualities. You have not understood that your worth and value are intrinsic to you. Even your physical and mental energy are valuable. It is your physical and mental energy that you exchange for money when you work. When you give your physical, mental, and emotional energy to your friends and family by being present for them, you are giving of your worth.

If you find that you are holding on to negative feelings about yourself you are probably favoring a pessimistic attitude about yourself. An optimistic attitude about yourself is more practical. Martin Seligman, PH.D., author of *Learned Optimism*, writes that optimistic attitudes and success are directly related.

A water glass is always both half empty and half full. Both of these perceptions are true. A pessimistic attitude is often thought of as practical. A pessimistic attitude assumes that a situation will worsen and the worst possible outcomes are most likely. The unfortunate thing about a pessimistic attitude is that it is a very limited way of looking at things. It will not see opportunities that could better the situation because it is not looking for these possibilities. With a narrowed focus on the negative, positive opportunities go unnoticed. To miss an opportunity to better a situation is extremely impractical.

The pessimistic side of us does need to be heard and acknowledged because it brings up concerns that need to be handled. Once we've opened a communication with our pessimistic side we can decide whether or not the pessimism has validity. Dr.

Seligman writes that there are certain situations where a pessimistic rather than an optimistic attitude is more appropriate. For example, if you were responsible for the safety of others, you would not optimistically take unnecessary risks.

If you have decided that the pessimistic messages you are giving yourself are unnecessary you can respond in a more optimistic, positive manner. On the other hand, if you continue with unnecessary pessimism you are severely limiting yourself. For example, if you are pessimistic about retiring early you won't seek out information on how to accomplish this. You won't ask someone who has succeeded how he or she did it. You'll assume the other person is lucky and you are not. With these assumptions you miss out on learning how you too might retire early. By limiting your ability to see opportunities pessimism becomes incredibly limiting. At the same time, optimism that does not heed the pessimistic side of us is equally limiting.

SECRET EIGHT ACTIONS

-1-

Look at the lists you made from Secrets Five and Seven. Relax your body and your mind. Allow yourself to breathe easily. Feel your natural connection to the Infinite Intelligence within you.

Take one item at a time and ask Infinite Intelligence to let you know the truth about this item, this belief. Ask Infinite Intelligence if you are seeing with the eyes of love or with the limited perception of a judgmental and critical self.

A new and more uplifting truth may come to you

immediately or may come later as a hunch, feeling, or dream. Perhaps a new truth will "occur" to you as you are talking to a friend or watching a movie. These are all ways that Infinite Intelligence communicates with you through your deeper self. When the new truth comes to you write it next to the negative belief on your list. Do this for each item on your lists.

For example, let's say that one of the items on your list is "I'm worthless."

After asking Infinite Intelligence for the truth about this attitude, you might realize that you have assumed you are worthless and have never acknowledged or admitted you have wonderful qualities. Your new truth might be "The truth is that I've ignored all of my fine qualities and refused to even acknowledge them."

-2-

When you have finished writing your new truths for each item on your lists, once again relax your body and mind. Allow yourself to breathe deeply and naturally. Feel your natural connection to your Infinite Intelligence.

Read the new truths you wrote for each item on your list. Feel the new truth in your body. Where do you feel this new truth in your body? What words describe the new feeling? Words like confidence, strength, opening, expansion, and well-being might describe the feeling you have when you feel your new truth.

Now remember the feelings in your body and the words that go with it. These feelings and words will be your reminder of the positive feelings of your new truth. By remembering the feelings in your body and the words that describe the experience you can have this uplifting feeling at any time.

For example, you might use the words, "deep happiness and confidence" and connect these words with an opening feeling in your chest and solar plexus. By remembering these physical feelings and your descriptive words you can experience the positive feeling of your new truth whenever you like. You will begin to see yourself more positively.

-3-

As you feel the new truth and remember it, at the same time imagine that your are releasing the old, negative belief or thought. Imagine that it slides off of you. Let go of your grasping and clinging to that negative attitude. As this old attitude slips off of you imagine the new you comes to the surface. Imagine this new you being filled with appreciation for yourself. Imagine this new you being confident that you can live your dream.

AFFIRMATIONS

The truth has now healed these old and limiting feelings, thoughts, attitudes and beliefs.

I now live my new and larger truth.

I now see myself more positively.

NOTES

SECRET NINE

Take action while being aware that you already
are and have what your heart desires.

Action or the activities you choose each day are
the connecting link between living your dream and
your everyday physical and material world. As you
focus your actions on living your dream it's important
to remind yourself that you are already whole and
complete.

When you desire something you assume that it
is separate from you. You need to remember that what
you dream of being or having is already part of you.
The image of what you desire is Infinite Intelligence

showing you your larger, more evolved self.

What you are really doing when you take action is allowing your more evolved self to emerge from inside of you. You are taking actions that will allow your more evolved self to express itself in the world.

Let's say that your dream is to play the violin. Your actions then would be ones that allow that more evolved self in you to express itself. You would perhaps buy a violin, find a teacher, and listen to great violinists. Your present self and your violinist self are not two separate people. Your musician self is your larger self waiting to express in the world.

When you realize that your violinist self is not separate from you this frees you from the anxiety that you are incomplete until you can play the violin well. Instead you will feel whole and fulfilled as you are becoming your new violinist self.

Remember, your deeper self listens to what you think and feel and takes these as directions. If you do not feel whole and complete your deeper self will manifest that state for you. As you take action each day always bear in mind that your heart's desire already exists within you as an image. This image is the seed that will emerge as your new self.

When you act as if you are already living your dream you are directing your deeper self to manifest your dream as a present reality. If you always think of your dream as a future event it will always seem just out of reach.

When you say "I Am" and "I Have" you are bringing your future self into your present reality. Secret Nine allows you to practice living your dream in the present. This practice will make your future self more and more natural to you. One day you will realize that the future self that you dreamed of has become your present self.

SECRET NINE ACTIONS

-1-

Fill in the blanks with your heart's desire:

I am_____now.

I have_____now.

As you take action each day hold these statements in your heart and mind. Act as if or pretend that you are living your dream now.

AFFIRMATIONS

Use the statements that you created in the Secret Nine Actions (above) as your affirmations.

NOTES

SECRET TEN

Realize that you are the expression of Infinite Intelligence.

You end where you began but on a higher spiral. In Secret One you realized your unity with Infinite Intelligence. Secret Ten now asks you to realize that you are Infinite Intelligence expressing itself in this world. It asks you to realize that through you Infinite Intelligence can take action in the world.

The dream you want to live, your heart's desire, is Infinite Intelligence revealing your greater, more evolved self to you. Infinite Intelligence is showing you how to allow it to manifest more fully in the world.

The closer you come to living your dream, the closer you are to fulfilling your divine potential, and the more Infinite Intelligence can bring heaven to earth. The *Bhagavad Gita,* one of India's greatest spiritual documents, teaches that the wise are those who allow the Infinite Intelligence to direct their lives. This is also a common theme in the Bible but it uses the term God for Infinite Intelligence. Many great religions and philosophies echo this idea as well.

When you live your dream Infinite Intelligence is working through you to prosper the world. By expressing itself through us Infinite Intelligence evolves us closer and closer to our divine potential. The world then becomes a better place.

As you live each of the Ten Secrets and realize that you are already what you dream of being, realize also that Infinite Intelligence is acting through you to prosper the world. When you live your dream you are making the world a better place.

SECRET TEN ACTIONS

-1-

Remind yourself that Infinite Intelligence is making the world a better place through you living your dream.

AFFIRMATIONS

Infinite Intelligence is expressing itself through me as I live my dream.

NOW YOU KNOW THE SECRETS

Congratulations, now you know the Ten Secrets of Living Your Dream. Read the Ten Secrets once a day until you remember them easily. Use your Manifesting Journal to record your progress. Make sure to date your entries. In the future when you review your Manifesting Journal you will be amazed at how your dreams became a reality.

Go through this book periodically to remind you of the details of the Secrets. Add your own insights and illuminations by writing them directly in the book. Practice the Secrets until you are living your dream.

The Ten Secrets are always happening in your life. You have now made them a conscious process. You will find your dreams and highest desires manifesting more easily now because you will have cleared many unconscious conflicts that have created obstacles for you in the past. Your dreams can now flow naturally into your real world. Be patient and consistent.

May your heaven come down to earth as you live your dream, and may you prosper us with your joyful contribution to our world.

THE TEN SECRETS OF LIVING YOUR DREAM

The terms "manifesting your heart's desire" and "living your dream" are used interchangeably. The heart uses dreams and daydreams to communicate its desires to us.

1. Realize your unity with Infinite Intelligence.

2. Decide on what your heart desires and make a commitment to living it.

3. Unify your conscious mind and your deeper self. Focus both of them on living your dream.

4. Imagine your dream is real now.

5. Choose your thoughts and what you say to yourself consciously.

6. Concentrate all of your actions on living your dream.

7. Realize what feelings and thoughts are keeping you from living your dream now.

8. Heal these negative feelings and thoughts by telling yourself the truth about them.

9. Take action while being aware that you already are and have what your heart desires.

10. Realize that you are the expression of Infinite Intelligence.

NOTES

BIBLIOGRAPHY

These are only a few of the hundreds of books that have contributed to formulating The Ten Secrets. These are some that have been particularly good friends in helping me to live my dreams.

Ashby, Muata. *Egyptian Yoga, The Philosophy of Enlightenment.* Miami, FL: Cruzian Mystic Books, 1995.

Andrews, Ted. *A Beginner's Guide to the New Age Qabalah.* St. Paul, MN: Llewellyn Publications, 1998.

Aurobindo, Sri. *The Synthesis of Yoga.* Pondicherry, India: All India Books, 1983.

Case, Paul Foster. *The Book of Tokens, Tarot Meditations.* Los Angeles, CA: Builders of the Adytum, 1989.

Case, Paul Foster. *The True and Invisible Rosicrucian Order.* York Beach, ME: Samuel Weiser, Inc., 1989.

Capra, Fritjof. *The Tao of Physics.* Boston, MA: Shambala Publications, 2000.

Chu, Chin-Ning. *Do Less, Achieve More.* NY, NY: Regan Books, 1998.

Easwaran, Eknath. *The Bhagavad Gita.* Tomales, CA: Nilgiri Press, 1999.

Easwaran, Eknath. *The Upanishads.* Tomales, CA: Nilgiri Press, 2000.

Fortune, Dion. *The Mystical Qabalah.* York Beach, ME: Samuel Weiser, Inc., 1984.

Hay, Louise. *You Can Heal Your Life.* Santa Monica, CA: Hay House, 1984.

Heisenberg, Werner. *Physics and Philosophy.* Amherst, NY: Prometheus Books, 1999.

Hulst, Dorothy. *As A Woman Thinketh.* Marina Del Rey, CA: DeVorss and Company Publishers, 1982.

Hoffman, Edward. *The Way of Splendor, Jewish Mysticism and Modern Psychology.* Boulder/London: Shambala, 1981.

Jampolsky, Gerald G. *Love Is Letting Go of Fear.* Berkeley/Toronto: Celestial Arts, 1988.

Jampolsky, Gerald G. *Out of the Darkness into the Light, A Journey of Inner Healing.* NY, Toronto, London, Sydney, Auckland: Bantam Books, 1990.

Jampolsky, Lee. *Healing the Addictive Mind.* Berkeley, CA: Celestial Arts, 1991.

Johnston, Charles. *The Yoga Sutras of Patanjali.* London: Stuart and Watkins, 1970.

King, Serge Kahili. *Kahuna Healing.* Wheaton, IL: Quest Books, Theosophical Publishing House, 1997.

Lotterhand, Jason C. *The Thursday Night Tarot Class.* North Hollywood, CA: Newcastle Publishing, 1989.

Mishra, M.D., Rammurti S. *The Textbook of Yoga Psychology. The Definitive Translation and Interpretation of Patanjali's Yoga Sutras.* NY, NY. Julian Press, 1987.

Orr, Leonard. *Breaking the Death Habit.* Berkeley, CA: Frog, Ltd., 1998.

Paramananda, Swami. *The Upanishads.* Cohasset, MA: Vedanta Center Publishers, 1981.

Ray, Sondra. *Loving Relationships.* Berkeley, CA. Celestial Arts, 1980.

Remele, Patricia. *Money Freedom.* Virginia Beach, VA: Association for Research and Enlightenment (A.R.E.), 1995.

Roberts, Jane. *The Individual and the Nature of Mass Events.* San Rafael, CA: Amber-Allen Publishing, 1995.

Roberts, Jane. *The Magical Approach.* Novato, CA: Amber-Allen Publishing, 1995.

Roberts, Jane. *The Nature of Personal Reality.* San Rafael/Novato CA: Amber-Allen Publishing, 1994.

Seligman, Martin E.P. *Learned Optimism.* NY, NY: Alfred A. Knopf, 1991.

Spangler, David. *Everyday Miracles.* NY, Toronto, London, Sydney, Auckland: Bantam Books, 1996.

Stanley, Thomas. *The Millionaire Mind.* Kansas City, MO: Andrews McMeel Publishing, 2000.

Sternberger, Robert J. *Successful Intelligence.* NY, NY: Plume, 1997.

Three Initiates. *The Kybalion, A Hermetic Philosophy of Ancient Egypt and Greece.* Chicago, IL: The Yogi Publication Society Masonic Temple, 1940.

Wing, R.L. *The I Ching Workbook.* Garden City, NY: Doubleday and Company, Inc., 1979.

Yogananda, Pramahansa. *The Autobiography of a Yogi.* Los Angeles, CA: Self-Realization Fellowship, 1998.

Zohar, Danah. *The Quantum Self.* NY, NY: Quill/William Morrow, 1990.

ORGANIZATIONS

Builders of the Adytum. 5101 North Figueroa St., Los Angeles, CA 90042. An organization dedicated to the Tradition of the Western Mysteries.

NOTES

ABOUT THE AUTHOR

Leyla Atwill has studied and practiced ancient and contemporary wisdom teachings for three decades. She is a practitioner of yoga and Qabalah. As a former registered nurse she specialized in psychiatry, was trained in hypnotherapy, and worked as a patient educator. She has worked with private clients in manifesting their heart's desire.

Atwill brings her insights to the steps needed in bringing one's highest vision to earth. She lives on the island of Maui in Hawaii with her husband, Frank, also a writer.

For information about ordering books, scheduling lectures or classes you can write or e-mail her at:

Leyla Atwill
P.O. Box 1622
Kihei, HI 96753

leylaatwill@yahoo.com

www.tensecrets.com

NOTES

ORDER FORM

Open a door for someone's dreams to come true. Give *The Ten Secrets of Living Your Dream* to a colleague or friend.

1 copy of The Ten Secrets of Living Your
Dream at regular price of $14.95   _____

10% DISCOUNT on 5 or more copies
Discounted price: $13.46 each

Send_____copies at $13.46   _____

SHIPPING and Handling:
Include $5.00 for one book plus $1.00
for each additional book   _____

SALES TAX:
Hawaii Residents must include sales
tax of 4.1%   _____

Payment by check or money order in
U.S. Funds. Allow 4-6 weeks for U.S.
orders. Allow more time for orders
outside the U.S.

TOTAL.....$_____

Make check payable to Leyla Atwill
Mail to: P.O. Box 1622
Kihei, HI 96753

Name_____

Address_____

_____

Phone_____E-mail_____

NOTES